Dear Parents and Educators,

Welcome to Penguin Young Readers! As parents and educators, you know that each child develops at his or her own pace—in terms of speech, critical thinking, and, of course, reading. Penguin Young Readers recognizes this fact. As a result, each Penguin Young Readers book is assigned a traditional easy-to-read level (1–4) as well as a Guided Reading Level (A–P). Both of these systems will help you choose the right book for your child. Please refer to the back of each book for specific leveling information. Penguin Young Readers features esteemed authors and illustrators, stories about favorite characters, fascinating nonfiction, and more!

Gorillas

LEVEL **3**

GUIDED READING LEVEL **L**

This book is perfect for a **Transitional Reader** who:
- can read multisyllable and compound words;
- can read words with prefixes and suffixes;
- is able to identify story elements (beginning, middle, end, plot, setting, characters, problem, solution); and
- can understand different points of view.

Here are some **activities** you can do during and after reading this book:
- Nonfiction: Nonfiction books deal with facts and events that are real. Talk about the elements of nonfiction. On a separate sheet of paper, write down the facts you learned about gorillas.
- Compound Words: A compound word is made when two words are joined together to form a new word. *Silverback* is a compound word that is used in this story. Reread the story and try to find other compound words.
- Research: Gorillas are endangered animals. Research what you and your friends and family can do to try to protect these animals.

Remember, sharing the love of reading with a child is the best gift you can give!

—Bonnie Bader, EdM
 Penguin Young Readers program

*Penguin Young Readers are leveled by independent reviewers applying the standards developed by Irene Fountas and Gay Su Pinnell in *Matching Books to Readers: Using Leveled Books in Guided Reading*, Heinemann, 1999.

To the Brennan champs,
Ryan and Kevin—PBD

In memory of my Uncle Ramon.

Special thanks to my brother Alfred
and my wife Rosa—PL

Special thanks to James G. Doherty,
General Curator, Bronx Zoo,
Wildlife Conservation Park.

Penguin Young Readers
Published by the Penguin Group
Penguin Group (USA) Inc., 375 Hudson Street, New York, New York 10014, USA
Penguin Group (Canada), 90 Eglinton Avenue East, Suite 700, Toronto, Ontario M4P 2Y3, Canada
(a division of Pearson Penguin Canada Inc.)
Penguin Books Ltd, 80 Strand, London WC2R 0RL, England
Penguin Ireland, 25 St Stephen's Green, Dublin 2, Ireland (a division of Penguin Books Ltd)
Penguin Group (Australia), 707 Collins Street, Melbourne, Victoria 3008, Australia
(a division of Pearson Australia Group Pty Ltd)
Penguin Books India Pvt Ltd, 11 Community Centre, Panchsheel Park, New Delhi—110 017, India
Penguin Group (NZ), 67 Apollo Drive, Rosedale, Auckland 0632, New Zealand
(a division of Pearson New Zealand Ltd)
Penguin Books, Rosebank Office Park, 181 Jan Smuts Avenue, Parktown North 2193, South Africa
Penguin China, B7 Jaiming Center, 27 East Third Ring Road North,
Chaoyang District, Beijing 100020, China

Penguin Books Ltd, Registered Offices: 80 Strand, London WC2R 0RL, England

Photo credits: pp. 3, 9, 10–11, 22, 23, 30, 31 © Gerry Ellis;
pp. 38–39, 43 © Ronald H. Cohn/The Gorilla Foundation.

Text copyright © 1994 by Patricia Brennan. Illustrations copyright © 1994 by Paul Lopez.
All rights reserved. First published in 1994 by Grosset & Dunlap, an imprint of Penguin Group (USA) Inc.
Published in 2013 by Penguin Young Readers, an imprint of Penguin Group (USA) Inc.,
345 Hudson Street, New York, New York 10014. Manufactured in China.

Library of Congress Control Number: 93039844

ISBN 978-0-448-40217-8   10 9 8 7 6

ALWAYS LEARNING   PEARSON

Gorillas

by Patricia Brennan Demuth
illustrated by Paul Lopez and with photographs

Penguin Young Readers
An Imprint of Penguin Group (USA) Inc.

King Kong crashes through
New York. He crushes cars.
People are screaming. Who can
stop this beast?

For many years, people believed gorillas were like King Kong in the movies. Scientists had not learned very much about gorillas. So no one knew the real facts.

Then, 54 years ago, a scientist named George Schaller moved to Africa. He wanted to live near gorillas. He wanted to watch gorillas up close. He found out that they are not terrible monsters—far from it. These giants of the jungle are shy and gentle.

Gorillas live in Africa. They make their homes in thick, rainy forests.

Some gorillas live in "lowlands" at sea level. They are called lowland gorillas.

Others live high in the mountains. And they are called mountain gorillas. Mountain gorillas have longer hair. That's because nights are cold in the mountains.

mountain gorilla

lowland gorilla

No matter where their homes are, gorillas live together in groups. They like company! Large groups may have 30 gorillas. Small groups may have only five.

The leader is an adult male called a silverback. He gets his name from the silver hair on his back. Silverbacks are huge.

Male gorillas weigh about 400 pounds and are nearly six feet tall. They can stretch their arms out eight feet wide.

Female gorillas are only about half the size of males.

The silverback is like a wise old king. He keeps order and peace in the group. These two gorillas are fighting over some food.

The silverback walks over and
stares at them. With just one look,
he ends the fight.

Sometimes the silverback will bark or grunt to stop a fight. He makes other sounds, too. Here, he whoops in surprise as a sunbird flies up from the path. All gorillas can make at least 25 sounds.

Each sound means something: a
hoot for alarm, a whimper for fear, a
roar for anger, a rumble for pleasure,
a purr for happiness.

The silverback decides everything for his group. Each day he decides when and where the group will go.

Gorillas are always on the move, looking for food. They walk one by one through the forest. At the head of the line is the silverback.

The silverback has found good
food. So the group stops to eat.
Gorillas don't eat any meat.

A good meal for a gorilla may be leaves, bark, fruit, or vines—with some wild celery for dessert!

Every afternoon the silverback stops the group for nap time.

Then just before dark, the group
stops again. This time they build
nests for sleeping. Gorillas make
their beds out of leaves and grass.
Some of the young nest in the trees.

The next morning, the gorillas
move on.

The beds will never be used again.

Anytime there is danger,
the silverback protects the
group. Here, a leopard comes
too close to a baby gorilla.
The baby's mother screams.

The silverback leaps up. He looks
huge! He hoots loudly. His teeth
flash in the sun. The silverback beats
his hands against his chest.

Then he charges with a roar. Not even a leopard will stay to fight. The leopard turns and runs away. The baby is safe.

Babies are very important to every
gorilla group. A mother gorilla
has only one baby at a time. Baby
gorillas are tiny at birth—only five
pounds. The mother carries the
baby everywhere.

Mother gorillas keep their babies close to them for three years.

They take good care of their babies. In a heavy rainstorm, a mother will hold her baby on her lap. She leans over the baby to keep it dry. But she gets soaking wet.

Young gorillas love to play.
They swing from one tree branch
to another,

roll around on the ground,

turn flips,

slide down hills,

and play tag.

One thing they can't do is swim.

Gorillas can't swim at all.

The adults are gentle with the young. They let the babies run around at nap time. And they often play games with the little ones.

This big male is tickling a baby
gorilla with a flower.

Sometimes it seems that gorillas have feelings like our own. Gorillas do belong to the same animal group that we do. The group name is primate.

squirrel monkey

chimpanzees

human

People, apes, and monkeys are all primates. Every primate has a big brain for its size. Our brain makes us able to think and to use words.

orangutan

gorilla

Scientists wanted to know if gorillas could learn to use words. The answer was yes. Koko was the first gorilla to "talk."

She learned sign language from her teacher, Penny Patterson. Now, Koko can make the signs for more than 600 words.

Koko "talks" even outside of class. If she is thirsty, she signs "drink." Sometimes Koko "talks" when she plays by herself.

Sometimes she spreads out her pink blanket. Then she makes the sign for "this pink." She picks up her doll and signs "baby."

Why can't Koko just say the words? Why does she have to sign? Gorillas can't talk because their mouths and tongues are not the right shape.

Besides being smart, Koko is very sensitive. When Penny laughs, Koko is happy. If Penny is hurt, Koko hugs her. One time Penny cried, and Koko licked away the tears. Koko also loves to play with kittens. She knows she must be gentle with them.

The more people learn about gorillas, the more amazing they seem. Yet one day there may be no gorillas left on earth.

Their forest homes are being
destroyed. Farms are taking their
place. Today, only a few hundred
mountain gorillas are left.

Some people are working hard to save these gentle beasts. Zoos and parks are raising lowland gorillas. Many keepers hope to return the gorillas to the wild someday.

Then the gorillas can be free in the forests again. They can live like they always have—on the move, in the open, close together.